T0197406

KiDS FOR SALE

Goat Kids, that is!

Sharon Marie Kraus

© Copyright 2021 Sharon Marie Kraus.

All rights reserved. No part of this publication may be reproduced, stored in a retrieval system, or transmitted, in any form or by any means, electronic, mechanical, photocopying, recording, or otherwise, without the written prior permission of the author.

Order this book online at www.trafford.com
or email orders@trafford.com

Most Trafford titles are also available at major online book retailers.

Trafford
PUBLISHING® www.trafford.com

North America & international
toll-free: 844 688 6899 (USA & Canada)
fax: 812 355 4082

Our mission is to efficiently provide the world's finest, most comprehensive book publishing service, enabling every author to experience success. To find out how to publish your book, your way, and have it available worldwide, visit us online at www.trafford.com

Because of the dynamic nature of the Internet, any web addresses or links contained in this book may have changed since publication and may no longer be valid. The views expressed in this work are solely those of the author and do not necessarily reflect the views of the publisher, and the publisher hereby disclaims any responsibility for them.

Any people depicted in stock imagery provided by Getty Images are models, and such images are being used for illustrative purposes only.
Certain stock imagery © Getty Images.

ISBN: 978-1-6987-0615-3 (sc)

ISBN: 978-1-6987-0616-0 (e)

Print information available on the last page.

Trafford rev. 03/02/2021

Kids For Sale. Goat kids, that is.

Goats have a lot of babies, called kids, and we can't keep them all.

Sometimes we have to find new homes for them. Luckily, other people want goats too, so when we sell them we can find them a good home.

There are many different breeds of goats.

Nubians have long floppy ears. They may be various shades and combinations of black, brown, white, cream, and grey. The British bred their goats with goats from Africa to get the Nubian goat.

Saanen goats are white or creamy white. They are from Switzerland and go to pastures in the high Alps like the movie 'Heidi'.

Toggenburgs are from Switzerland too. They are always the same shade of brown, with facial stripes and ears that stand up.

Boer goats are larger bodied goats. They are meat goats and their meat is called chevon. They are white and reddish brown.

Angora goats have beautiful curly hair that is called
mohair. It is very soft and can be spun into yarn.

Here is an Angora goat after being shorn. Their hair will grow back quickly. If it gets cold we put them in the barn with a heat lamp, and put on old sweatshirt on them. We added a string of pearls on this goat for a fun picture.

This is a herd of Angora goats. Some people keep guard dogs like this Great Pyrenees with their goats to protect them.

Nigerian Dwarf goats are a smaller breed and are
nice size goats for children to handle.

Most goats produce milk after they have their babies.
They are milked on a milking stand. Toggenburgs, Nubians,
Sanaans, Alpines, and La Manchas are all good milkers.

Goats provide very good milk for people. Many things will determine how much milk you will get. A few of those things are, the breed of the goat, what she eats, if she drinks plenty of fresh water, and her age.

The milk can be used for drinking, making cheese, yogurt, ice cream and lots of other good things. There are a lot of good books for recipes using goats' milk and other helpful information on milking.

Goats are herd animals and love to be with their families. They also like being with other goats and making friends with other farm animals.

They love their human friends the best. And we love them!

Goats need people to take care of them. They need shelter with fences that keep them safe from predators. Goats need good hay, grain, and clean water. They need to be groomed and have their hooves trimmed. Most important, goats need companionship.

Male, or boy goats, are called bucks.

Female, or girl goats, are called does.

When they have a baby, it is called a kid. A baby goat will nurse from its mother until it is old enough to eat grass and grain. Mother goats love their babies and take very good care of them.

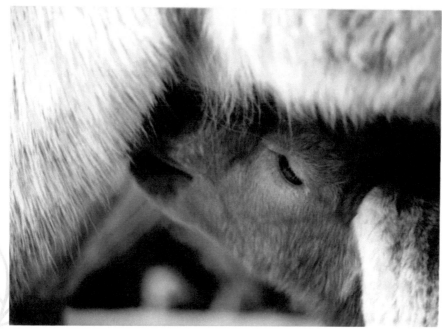

Goats like to eat almost anything that grows outside.
They love leaves and all my flowers.

Goats are very playful and they love to run, climb, and jump. They like to butt heads with each other. They are always up to something mischievous.

Goats are curious and personable. They do a lot of silly things.
They are fun to watch and give us lots of laughs.

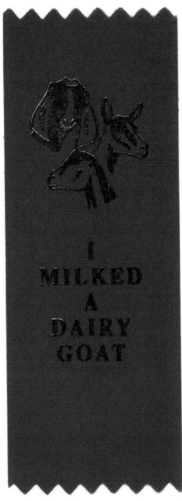

Grape
Ice Cream

I
MILKED
A
DAIRY
GOAT

There are a lot of things you can do with goats. You can take them
to petting zoo's and let other's try milking a goat. We give ribbons
to kids who try milking our goat. You can take them in parades.
We had a recipe for Grape Ice Cream in the Grape Festival
Parade. All the children love playing with and seeing goats.

You can take a goat to a 4-H or goat show. When they are all cleaned up they are elegant and sleek, a lot like deer.

It takes practice handling your goat if you want to take it
to a goat show. The goat has to be able to stand still when
you ask them to and walk where you want them to go. They
will have to be able to be around others and behave.

We hope if you get a goat, that you will always have as much fun with your goat as we've had with ours.

Vocabulary

Boer - a breed of goat used for meat.

Breed - a group of animals with similar characteristics that distinguish it.

Buck - an adult male goat

Buckling - a young male goat

Caprine - a scientific name for the goat species.

Chevon - a French word for goat meat.

Doe - an adult female goat sometimes called nanny goat.

Doeling - a young female goat.

Fiber goat - goats that have hair that can be harvested and used for textile production.

Forage - the hay or grassy portion of the goats diet.

Freshen - when a doe gives birth (or kids) and starts to produce milk.

Kid - a goat less than one year old.

Lactation - the period in which a doe produces milk.

Milk stand or stanchion - a place the does stands while being milked.

Nutrition - the level of specific nutrients needed to keep an animal healthy and productive, and how to provide those nutrients.

Sire - a male parent.

Udder - the mammary gland of a goat that secretes milk.

Wattle - a small appendage attached on or near the throat of a goat.

Weanling - a young goat who has stopped suckling or nursing its mother.

Wether - a male goat that has been castrated.

Yearling - a male or female goat that it between one and two years old.

Grape Ice Cream

2 cups heavy cream, 1 ¼ cups grape juice, 1/3 cup sugar, ¼ teaspoon salt. You can also add lemon juice or lemon zest if you like. Stir and freeze according to ice cream freezer directions or fill a large plastic bag with ice and salt. Then put your ice cream mix in a smaller plastic bag and put the small bag into the big bag of ice. Shake for awhile till the ice cream mix is cold enough to turn into ice cream.

Queso Blanco Cheese

Queso Blanco cheese is a Latin American cheese. The names means white cheese.

Warm one gallon of milk to 180 degrees. Stir often so it doesn't scorch. Keep it at 180 degrees for several minutes. Slowly add ¼ cup vinegar until curds separate from the whey. Pour everything into a cheesecloth lined colander to strain. Tie the four corners together and hang to drain for several hours, till the bag of cheese stops dripping. Your cheese will then be a solid cheese that can be put in a container and kept refrigerated for up to a week.

Reference/Resources

American Dairy Goat Association

Dairy Goat by Diana Grocery

Raising Milk Goats Successfully by Gail Luttman

Raising Milk Goats the Modern Way by Jerry Belanger

Dairy Goat for Pleasure and Profit by Harvey Considine

Goat keeping 101 - Caprine Supply 800-646-7736 for a free catalogue containing goat and milking supplies.

Cheese making Made Easy bu Ricki & Robert Carroll

Goats Produce Too by Mary Jane Toth.

www.Redsidedairygoats.com Breeders of Nigerian Dwarf Goats

About the Book

Goats make great pets. They are friendly and playful. They are also useful. They give milk, meat or mohair for yarn. They are good companions for people and other animals.

About the Author

The author has spent years raising goats and other farm animals. She finds a lot of happiness caring for them. She shared her love of animals with her six children. In this book, she and her children, and friends share some of their fun experiences with their goats.

Printed in the United States
By Bookmasters